D0500196

TEACHERS

THE STRUGGLE IS REAL.

Math

Lesson Plans

Inspiring | Educating | Creating | Entertaining

Brimming with creative inspiration, how-to projects, and useful information to enrich your everyday life, Quarto Knows is a favorite destination for those pursuing their interests and passions. Visit our site and dig deeper with our books into your area of interest: Quarto Creates, Quarto Cooks, Quarto Homes, Quarto Lives, Quarto Drives, Quarto Explores, Quarto Gifts, or Quarto Kids.

Text © 2017 by Bored Teachers LLC Art © Creative Market

This edition published in 2019 by Crestline, an imprint of
The Quarto Group 142 West 36th Street, 4th Floor New York, NY 10018 USA
T (212) 779-4972 **F** (212) 779-6058 **www.QuartoKnows.com**

First published in 2017 by Rock Point, an imprint of The Quarto Group,
142 West 36th Street, 4th Floor, New York, NY 10018, USA

Crestline titles are also available at discount for retail, wholesale, promotional, and bulk purchase. For details, contact the Special Sales Manager by email at specialsales@quarto.com or by mail at The Quarto Group, Attn: Special Sales Manager, 100 Cummings Center, Suite 265-D, Beverly, MA 01915, USA.

10 9 8 7 6 5 4 3 2

ISBN: 978-0-7858-3772-5

Editorial Director: Rage Kindelsperger
Creative Director and Cover Designer: Merideth Harte
Interior Design: Nina Simoneaux
Managing Editor: Erin Canning
Editorial Project Manager: Chris Krovatin

Printed in Singapore COS072020

This book provides a humorous view into the lives of teachers. It does not seek to provide any information about education, education laws and regulations, or teaching requirements in any state or country.

TEACHERS

THE STRUGGLE IS REAL

Math

Lesson Plans

HISTORY

Glitterholic!

BY *Bored Teachers*

CRESTLINE

TABLE OF CONTENTS

Chapter	1	Back to School	7
Chapter	2	Classroom Life: Behind the Lesson Plan	17
Chapter	3	Admin, Meetings, and All That Good Stuff	27
Chapter	4	We're In It for the Money	37
Chapter	5	Surviving the Holidays	47
Chapter	6	School Supplies	59
Chapter	7	Climbing Paperwork Mountain	69
Chapter	8	Weekend Madness	81
Chapter	9	The End Is Near	93
Chapter	10	Summer Break . . . Because We Deserve It!	103
Chapter	11	How Much We Love These Kids	115

CHAPTER I
BACK TO SCHOOL

The start of a new school year is an emotional roller coaster for teachers. We dread the end of summer but are excited to meet our new kids. We don't want the barbecues and poolside days to end, but our classrooms won't decorate themselves! School supply sections taunt us every time we walk in any store. It's back to the drawing board, back to reality, the dreamy time of summer break is over. Heigh-ho, it's back to school we go!

First day of school

vs.

Every other day of school

EAGERNESS
EXCITEMENT
FEAR
STRESS
PANIC ATTACKS
DENIAL

The different stages of going back to school.

A well-decorated classroom is just like the smile on my face. It makes everyone feel a little safer, even though there's an overwhelming mess behind it.

THE MORE STUDENTS
THE MERRIER!

-said no teacher ever.

I don't know what's better,
finding out your class list is shorter
than the year before or getting paid for
all the overtime hours you put in.

Who cares!
Neither is ever going to happen.

Every year, I wonder if this will be the last year I get a knot in my stomach walking into school on the first day back.

BACK TO SCHOOL

When teachers transform into balls of anxiety every Sunday night.

THE COPY ROOM

where teachers transform into merciless, selfish monsters.

Dear Admin,

Thanks again for another productive staff meeting, where everything we discussed was about the next meeting.

Teaching your students not to be jealous of others, but secretly hating the teacher next door for having such a cool-looking classroom.

Q: What's worse than getting a new student added to your roster after you've just finished labelling everything?

A: Maybe staff meetings. Yeah, staff meetings are worse.

CHAPTER 2

CLASSROOM LIFE:
BEHIND THE LESSON PLAN

The classroom is a mystical place where total pandemonium is brewed into progress and where dreams come true. It's a place where nothing makes sense until everything makes sense. It's a place where shyness becomes confidence, fear becomes courage, and readers become leaders. It's where the definition of chaotic-struggle is found, and the teacher is the maestro of it all.

AND SO IT BEGINS!

People say your prime age is your 30s.
I still believe that your prime age
is during kindergarten, when you
get applauded for coloring shapes,
singing the alphabet, and taking naps.

Teacher Odds:

CHANCES OF EVER BEING RICH.

 =

CHANCES OF NOT HAVING TO TAKE WORK HOME.

You know the frustration of putting a fitted sheet on a king-size bed by yourself? Or how about trying to pick an ice cube off the kitchen floor? Well, combine them and multiply by 50.

That's what just the first few hours in a day of teaching feels like.

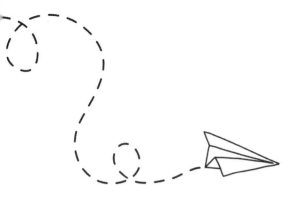

Dear Teacher,

I don't understand how my son got a "C" on this project. I spent like 5 hours on it!

Sincerely,

A Very "Concerned" Parent

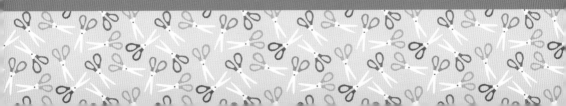

If you can survive a month straight of

INDOOR RECESS

without losing your mind,

you've achieved

SAINTHOOD

TEACHING PRO TIP

When you get a chance to pee without leaving your class unsupervised, you take it!

My students call me the teacher,
but I like to think of myself as

"BREEDER OF TOMORROW'S LEADERS."

Just sounds more precise.

I'm not sure what's worse:

touching something wet in your classroom and not knowing what it is, or touching something sticky on a homework assignment and not knowing what it is.

They should make a new *Survivor* episode, where they lock contestants in a room with 50 children during indoor recess, on the day of a full moon.

TEACHER CONFESSION

50% of teaching young kids is saying things that should never be said out loud, by any human being, such as, "Get your toes out of your mouth!"

CHAPTER 3

ADMIN, MEETINGS, AND ALL THAT GOOD STUFF

Anyone who has ever stood in a classroom, in front of a group of kids from different backgrounds, with different learning needs, knows that teaching is not an easy job. Throw in some random observations, endless staff meetings, piles of paperwork, helicopter parents, and a salary based on test scores...and you'll start to understand the true meaning of "Teacher Struggle".

If teachers had thought bubbles over their heads during staff meetings:

If she asks one more question, I swear to . . .
I WONDER IF I CAN FALL ASLEEP WITH MY EYES OPEN . . .
Should I have pizza or tacos tonight?

The Sound of Teaching:
My Least Favorite Things

Sub plans on sick days,
and meetings on Mondays . . .

Jammed copy machines,
and grading on Sundays . . .

Indoor recess with no
playground swings,

These are a few of my
least favorite things!

Teaching is the most rewarding job in the world.

Except when parent-teacher conferences, report cards, a full moon, and a PD meeting all happen during the week before Thanksgiving break.

TEACHER'S FAVORITE FAIRY TALE

Once upon a time, admin didn't add any more students to my class after I already finished laminating the class list and all my labels.

The end.

Dear Mrs. Smith,

Your classroom management skills have exceeded our expectations this year. Fantastic work. To show our appreciation, we've decided to add a few more students to your class so you can continue to make a difference in more kids' lives.

Kind regards,
Admin

P.S. Oh, and if any of them fails the end-of-the-year exams, we'll reduce your salary by 10% next year.

Dear Admin,

Thank you for switching me to a
different grade, right after I
started feeling comfortable, and
spent 2 years of my career creating
lesson plans and classroom materials
that will now be completely useless.

Sincerely,

No Teacher Ever

Long weekends with no papers to grade are to happiness as after-school faculty meetings are to _____.

a) Torture
b) Hell
c) Misery
d) Depression
e) All of the above

CHAPTER 4

WE'RE IN IT FOR THE MONEY

It's been said that teachers make as many decisions on a minute-to-minute basis as a brain surgeon. So why is it that most teachers make less than a cable TV installer? Teachers are faced with one of society's most important tasks every day, yet we're constantly asked to give more of our time for less and less money. Nonetheless, we get up every day and try to change the world one student at a time. Our bank accounts may be empty, but our hearts are full of love and laughter!

TEACHERS

The only human beings who would buy a new set of markers before paying their bills.

TEACHER PAYCHECK

A reminder that you chose to give more than you'll ever make.

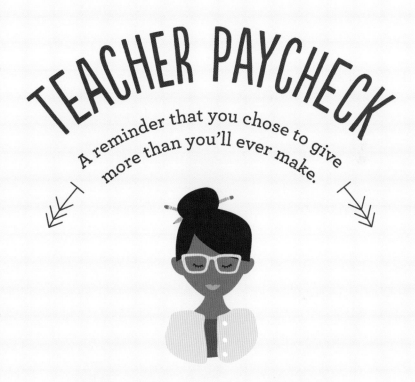

EVERY TIME I GET MY PAYCHECK . . .

...it reminds me that this gig is all about the kids.

...my bank account laughs at me.

My car needs new tires, my electric bill is overdue, and my fridge has no food in it. But at least my bulletin board matches the new cubbyholes in my classroom!

PRiORiTiES.

Tying the salaries of teachers to the results of standardized tests sounds like a wonderful idea. While we're at it, let's add a disclaimer to each test that reads:

"With every mistake, a teacher's job is at stake."

I wish they would evaluate my performance on my teaching skills, instead of through test scores.

You know, like being awesome at reading and writing upside down.

I teach for the:

~~BIG SALARY~~
~~ABUNDANCE OF~~
~~FREE TIME~~
~~CONSTANT~~
~~MEETINGS~~
KIDS

I teach for the kids.

ME:
"I need a vacation
on a quiet,
little island,
with a book in
one hand and
a margarita
in the other . . ."

MY BANK ACCOUNT:
"HAHAHAHAHAHAHAHA"

Teaching is the only profession in which someone would hoard empty toilet-paper rolls for an entire year because craft supplies are outside the school's budget.

ME EVERY MORNING:

"I seriously need some new clothes!"

ME AT THE STORE:

"Oh, laminators are on sale though . . ."

CHAPTER 5

SURVIVING THE HOLIDAYS

For most people, the holidays bring back
fond memories of joyous celebrations
and jolly spirits. For teachers, the holidays
are hard work. Children are off the walls,
school events cut into the million things
we need to get done, our classrooms
need to be RE-decorated, and our
endurance is put to the test.

HALLOW-THANKS-MAS:

When Halloween, Thanksgiving, and

Christmas feel like one big, painful

blur that never seems to end.

Every Halloween, I prevent more cavities than a dentist with the amount of candy I confiscate and devour.

THE HALLOWEEN QUESTION:

How long is long enough before I can eat an unclaimed, confiscated piece of chocolate?

NOVEMBER 1, 12:01 A.M.

the Christmas season officially begins.

Brace yourselves . . .

Chaos is coming.

You think holiday questions from
family you haven't seen
in a year are bad . . .

Try standing in front of a room
full of children asking you every
personal question imaginable.

MIGRAINE:

Teaching during the first 3 weeks of December leading up to Christmas.

Christmas stopped being my favorite holiday the day I realized I would have to choreograph a Nativity play with 50 uncontrollable tiny humans, jacked up on candy canes...

EVERY. SINGLE. YEAR.

Being a teacher
the week before any
HOLIDAY BREAK
is comparable to being
A ZOOKEEPER
in a cage-free zoo.

I'd say I have a pretty balanced diet . . .

On most days of the year, my lunches consist
of a sandwich, a salad, a yogurt, or fruit . . .

Around the holidays, they consist of confiscated
candy, cookies from the break room, and leftover
cupcakes from classroom parties.

IT'S A SOLID BALANCE.

"OK, class, we're going to play a game called **Wax Museum.** You have to pretend to be a wax statue, and I'll be the security guard of the museum. If I see you move or hear you make a noise, you lose,"

said every clever teacher, the day before Christmas break.

Most of the year,
I'm a manager, a therapist,
a mediator, a nurse,
and an actor.

In December, it's all about
CROWD CONTROL.

TEACHER CHRISTMAS CAROL

"It's the most wonderful time, of the year . . . to sleep!"

CHAPTER 6

SCHOOL SUPPLIES

Every teacher knows that going into a classroom without the proper supplies is like a soldier going to war without a gun. It's dangerous. School supplies are the tools we need for the job. The better the school supplies, the more prepared we are. The more prepared we are, the fewer headaches we get. The fewer headaches we get, the less wine we drink. You get the point. School supplies are important.

OK, fine, maybe we're just addicted . . .

So what!

I'M A GLITTER-HOLIC.

I know how much of a mess it will make.

I know I'll never be able to get it out of anything I own.

I know it will eventually make me lose my mind.

BUT I JUST CAN'T HELP MYSELF.

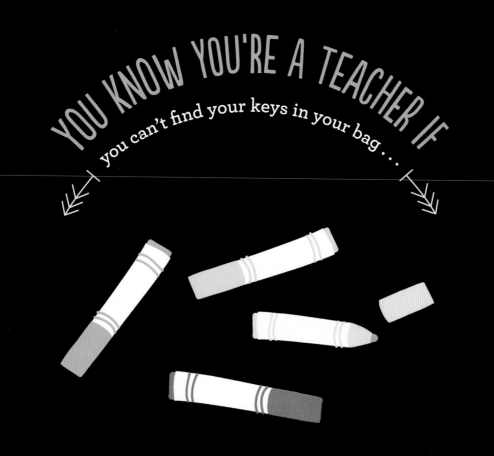

YOU KNOW YOU'RE A TEACHER IF

you can't find your keys in your bag . . .

. . . because they're buried under
a pile of dried-up whiteboard markers.

"I never run out of pencils in my classroom," said no human teacher ever, in the history of mankind.

- **Number of pencils in my classroom on the first day of school: 500**

- **Number of pencils in my classroom during the second week of school: 20**

- **Number of pencils in my classroom not chewed on: 0**

- **Percentage of parents complaining I don't provide enough supplies: 98%**

What's little, orange, and disappears more than socks in the laundry and Tupperware lids in the kitchen?

THE TOPS TO GLUE STICKS!

It's important for teachers to step back and think about all the consequences before doing something that could have disastrous repercussions . . .

You know, like taking out the glitter.

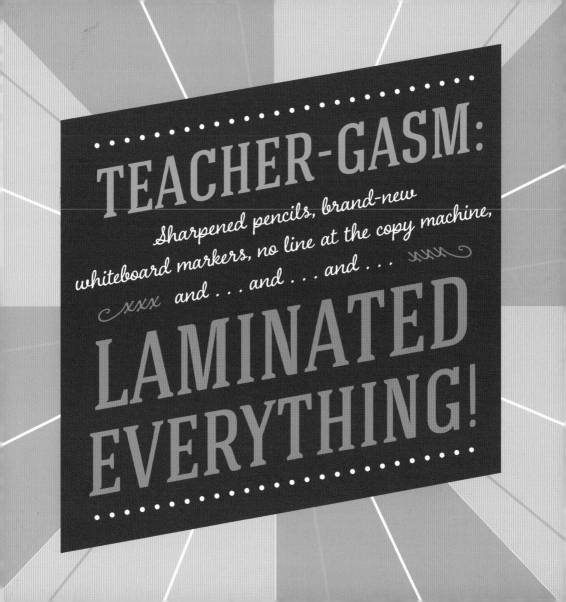

FIRST DAY OF SCHOOL:

**My pencils are for you to
BORROW for 2 purposes ONLY:
Writing and erasing
IN MY CLASSROOM.**

That's it!

NOT for teething, NOT for itching your back,
NOT for playing the drums on your desk, NOT for cleaning
your ears, NOT for poking your neighbor, NOT for flicking
spitballs across the room, NOT for bathroom graffiti,
NOT for carving "I ♥ Mary" into school property.
DO NOT sharpen while I'm giving instructions.
DO NOT add them to the collection of stolen school
supplies in your bookbags.

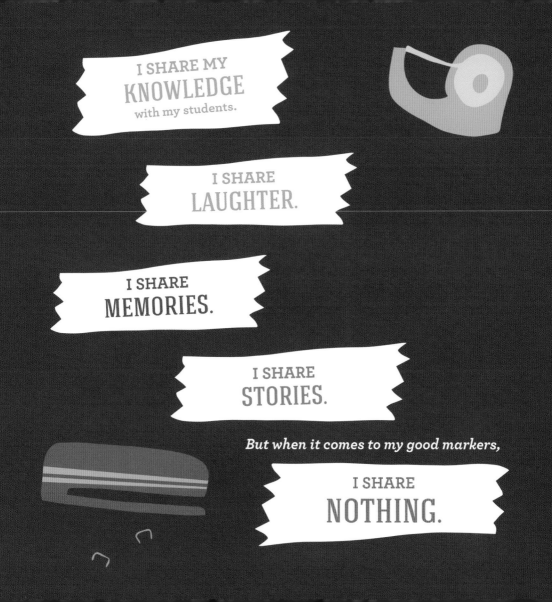

I SHARE MY
KNOWLEDGE
with my students.

I SHARE
LAUGHTER.

I SHARE
MEMORIES.

I SHARE
STORIES.

But when it comes to my good markers,

I SHARE
NOTHING.

CHAPTER 7

CLIMBING PAPERWORK MOUNTAIN

With the never-ending tests comes the never-ending cycle of grading. But with the amount of other responsibilities and tasks to accomplish, the papers easily pile up. Throw all the assignments, worksheets, photocopies, and lesson plans on top, and that paper pile quickly becomes a paper mountain that consumes your social life, your Sunday nights, and your sanity!

Essential tools for grading papers:

1. PAJAMAS
2. SNACKS
3. COMFY CHAIR
4. COFFEE/TEA/BEER/WINE
5. RED PEN
6. NETFLIX
7. PHONE TO CALL TEACHER FRIEND

FRIEND: Hey, what are you doing this weekend?

ME: Oh, just writing lesson plans for 40 kids with different learning abilities, different learning styles, and different family/cultural backgrounds, all while making sure they pass the standardized tests that determine my value to the school.

Otherwise, not much.

Logic 101

❧

If parents can complain about the amount of homework we give students, then teachers should be able to complain to admin about the amount of paperwork we're forced to do at home.

ESSENTIAL SCHOOL SUPPLIES THAT TEACHERS SHOULD NEVER HAVE TO PAY FOR:

- Dry-erase markers
- Red pens
- Pencils
- Aspirin
- Chocolate
- Coffee/tea/wine

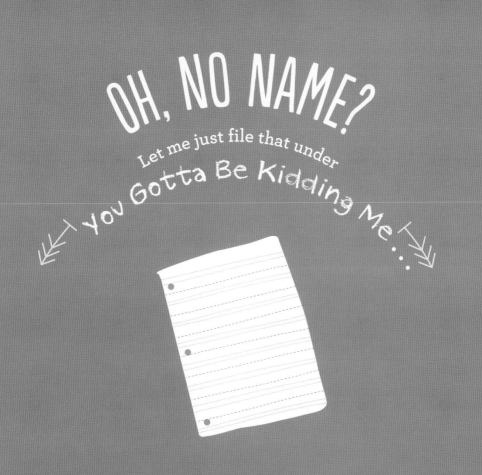

I guess you can say today was a pretty successful day. I disassembled the mountain of paperwork on my desk, stuck it in the trunk of my car, went home, made tacos, and fell asleep before 9:00 p.m. . . .

Making tacos and falling asleep before 9:00 p.m. was obviously the successful part.

"I don't have any bags big enough to carry home all the papers I need to grade this weekend,"

SAID EVERY TEACHER . . . EVERY FRIDAY AFTERNOON.

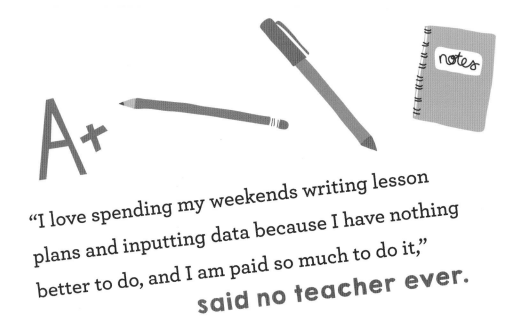

"I love spending my weekends writing lesson plans and inputting data because I have nothing better to do, and I am paid so much to do it," **said no teacher ever.**

You know what's worse than having a 103-degree fever, sore throat, sinus congestion, deep cough, runny nose, upset stomach, headache, chills, and nausea?

Trying to find a sub and writing sub plans while having all of the above.

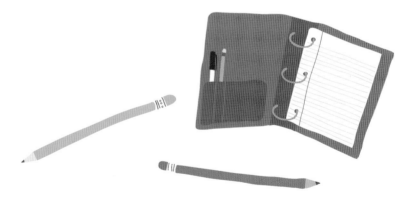

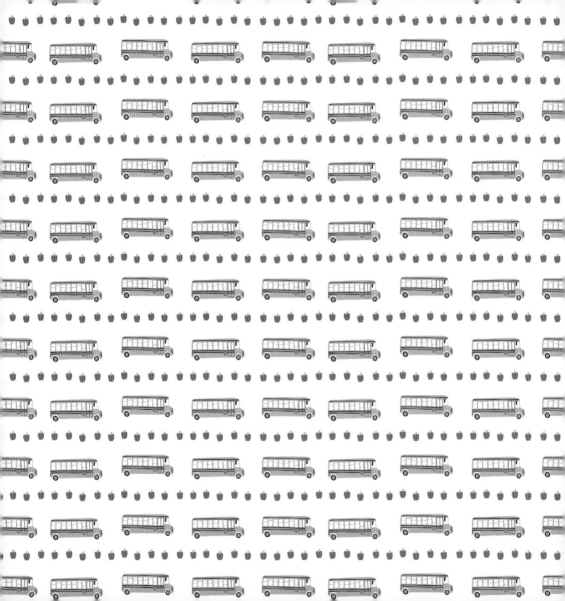

CHAPTER 8

WEEKEND MADNESS

When the Monday to Friday struggle ends, we get 2 days to recharge our batteries before Monday comes back and slaps us across the face. But for teachers, the weekends aren't all they're cracked up to be. They fly by and there's barely any leisure time to rest and recuperate. Eventually, Sunday night arrives, and the anxiety comes charging back. Lesson plans need to be made, papers need to be graded, and laundry needs to be done. Teacher life has no time for rest!

If you're not into

SOCIALIZING

you should try teaching. Spending
the weekend grading and lesson
planning is where it's at!

PANTY SHOPPING PHOBIA (PSP)

The fear of running into a student while shopping for new underwear.

SUNDAY NIGHT SYNDROME (SNS)

The fear of going back to school on Monday morning.

TEACHER HANGOVER

Waking up after a long night of grading lousy papers, and feeling hopeless for the future of humanity.

- "Yay! It's finally the weekend. I can't wait to catch up with all my friends.

- And by friends, of course, I mean all the grading I haven't done over the last 2 months."

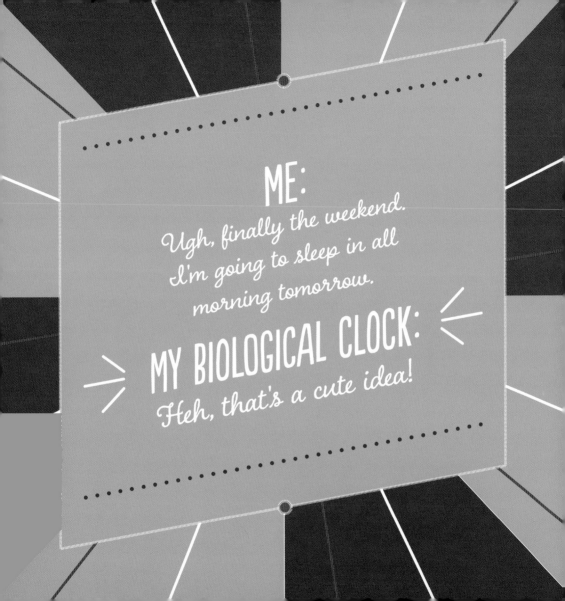

The biggest lie I tell myself is:

"I'M GOING TO CATCH UP ON ALL MY GRADING THIS WEEKEND."

TEACHER SAFETY

What to do if you see a student or parent at the store over the weekend:

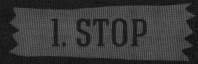 **1. STOP** Stop where you are.

Drop to the ground. 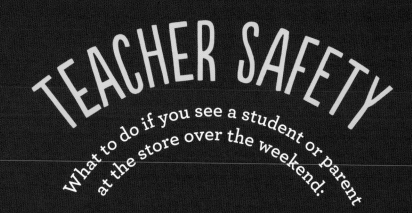 **2. DROP**

 **3. ROLL** Cover your face with hands and roll over.

Going out and meeting new people is cool.

But have you tried curling up on the couch in your PJs at 7:00 p.m. with a cup of tea, so you can wake up early and write lesson plans on Sunday morning?

There are 3 things I look forward to on the weekends:

1. TURNING OFF MY ALARM CLOCK

2. SLEEPING

3. PRETENDING I'M NOT AN ADULT

"I can't wait to spend the weekend writing lesson plans because of the mandatory staff meetings scheduled during all my prep time!"
-said no teacher ever.

WORD TO THE WISE

If you go out on the weekends with teacher friends, there's a 98% chance the main topic of conversation will be about classroom shenanigans and school gossip.

CHAPTER 9

THE END IS NEAR

If you manage to survive December, guess what, you're not even halfway there! By the time Spring Break hits, you're ready to go wild. And by wild, of course, I mean catch up on all the paperwork and lost hours of sleep. The rest of the year is a struggle, a battle with time and daydreamers. That sweet smell of summer starts taking over your students' minds like a hypnotic spell, drifting them further and further away from the desire to learn. May the force be with you.

"911, please state your emergency."

"Yeah, hi, I'd like to report an attempted murder. My school calendar says there aren't any breaks or days off in March."

Imagine climbing a

MOUNTAIN

— with a 100-pound backpack. That last — 100-feet before you get to the top? That's what

TEACHING IN MAY

feels like.

"It's been one of

THOSE DAYS

for like 9 months now," says every teacher in May.

By June, all school
break rooms should be required by law to have

A MARGARITA MACHINE.

I BECAME A TEACHER TO MAKE A DIFFERENCE IN THE WORLD.

But in reality, I'm just happy to make it through each day without having a mental breakdown.

HOW TO IDENTIFY A TEACHER IN JUNE:

- Double-fists coffee mugs.
- Stares at clock more than students.

SUMMER BREAK IS COMING

and all my students are asking me
where I'm going on vacation...

ZZZ
ZZZ
ZZZ
ZZZ
ZZZ

MY RESPONSE:

"BED. I'M GOING TO BED."

During the months of May and June, I contemplate daily whether I need an IV of coffee, a flask in my classroom desk drawer, a steady diet of tacos and pizza, or 6 months of sleep.

PROBABLY ALL OF THE ABOVE.

· · · · · · ·   ✕   · · · · · · ·

At the end of the school year, I don't have any ducks in a row. They're more like pigeons who've been force-fed speed pills at a rave party.

I DON'T KNOW WHAT'S WORSE:

being observed during the last 3 weeks of school or

RUNNING INTO A PARENT

≥ *at the* ≤

LIQUOR STORE.

How to make it through the end of the school year:

1. Drink a ridiculous amount of caffeine.
2. Learn how to take naps with your eyes open during staff meetings.

TEACHER-IN-MAY INSTINCT:

Involuntarily punching someone in the face who says "Teachers shouldn't complain. They get the summer off!" during the month of May.

Chapter 10

SUMMER BREAK...
BECAUSE WE DESERVE IT!

Ah, summer break... when teachers get the opportunity
to feel like normal human beings again. It's the time when
teachers get to collect on all the overtime hours they put in
during the school year. It's a time to relax and
recharge the batteries, to prepare for shaping the
minds of another group of future leaders.
Summer break is important!

The only thing worse than
an unannounced observation
is an observation during
summer school.

Summertime

Time to sleep without
anything on your mind.

Time to chew your food
before you swallow it.

And time to sneeze without
the fear of wetting your pants.

When I wake up during summer break,
I lie in bed and laugh to myself for a
moment, imagining all the parents with
their children all day, every day.

Summer break is like one long
weekend for teachers, and one long
teacher appreciation day for parents.

THIS WINE PAIRS PERFECTLY

with not having any grading to do, and not having to take care of everyone else's kids all summer.

My biggest fears:

1. Giant spiders
2. Scary clowns
3. Running into students at places
   I like going to during the summer

"UH OH . . ."

says every teacher looking at their bank account at the end of summer.

SUMMER | When teachers have zero recollection of which day of the week it is. And that is bliss. Pure bliss.

Summer luxuries of a teacher:

1. PEEING WHENEVER YOU WANT

2. DRINKING COFFEE BEFORE
   IT GETS COLD

3. READING A BOOK NOT
   WRITTEN FOR CHILDREN

4. NO BELLS, NO FIRE DRILLS,
   NO ALARM CLOCKS

5. SILENCE . . . SWEET SILENCE

SUMMER

The only time of year teachers don't have to plan a schedule for when they can drink water.

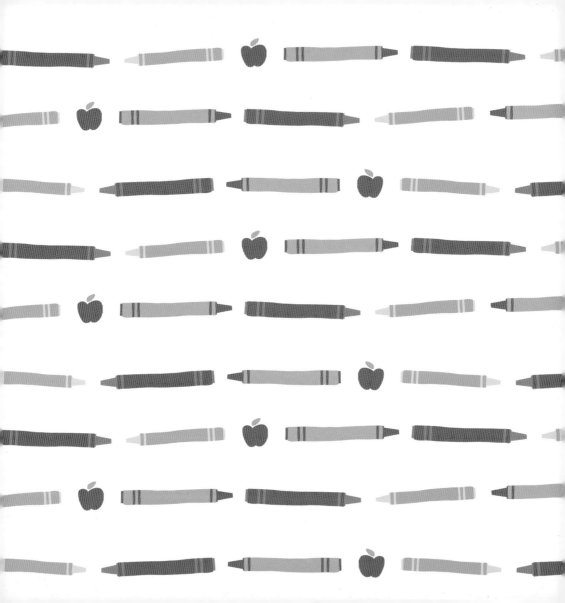

Chapter 11

HOW MUCH WE LOVE THESE KIDS

It's all about the kids. Teaching is always all about the kids. We deal with all the sweat, tears, stress, headaches, and mental breakdowns, because we believe we serve a purpose much larger than us. Teaching is not for everyone. It takes a special type of person to handle the utter chaos and misery that comes with the job. But we do it for the difference we make in so many children's lives every single day. And even when they push us to our very limits, to the point where we lose our minds, our social life, and any youth left in us, we find a way to laugh about it, vent about it, and keep going.

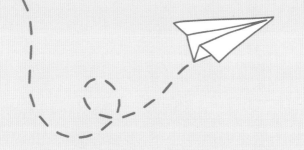

Teaching is the only profession
that makes you reconsider ever
having children of your own.

You know that saying "He's a chip off the old block?"

Well, you'll never know how profound that truly is until you've sat on the teacher side of a parent-teacher meeting.

Deciding on the seating arrangement
is like playing chess against a master chess
player . . . who has twice as many pieces
as you, and you only have pawns left.

Every move must be overanalyzed
or you're in trouble!

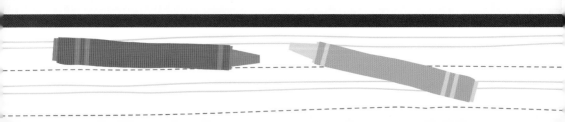

Some days, my students are the reason I get out of bed in the morning. Other days, my students are the reason I remain in bed for as long as humanly possible.

Zzz
Zzz
Zzz

You know what they say . . .
What happens in my
classroom, stays in my . . .

MIND.

All night. And doesn't allow me to fall
asleep until I figure out how to make it
better, or cuter, or more efficient.

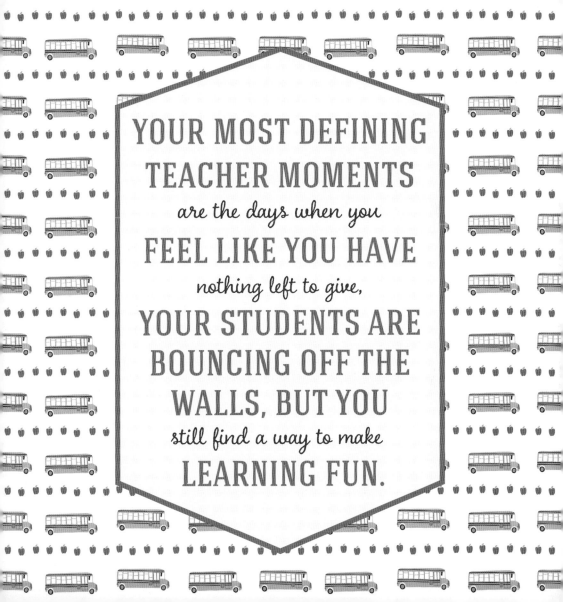

TEACHING IS LIKE READING A BOOK:

...while skydiving, during a thunderstorm, over the ocean, in the middle of the night, unsure if your chute is going to open.

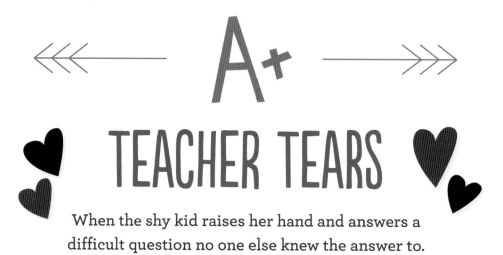

A+

TEACHER TEARS

When the shy kid raises her hand and answers a difficult question no one else knew the answer to.

There are days when my students remind me why I became a teacher . . . And there are days when they remind me to buy more wine and aspirin after school.

There is only one thing slower than the line at airport security . . .

A kid on his way back to your classroom when you let him go to the bathroom.

The most common thought in a teacher's mind during parent-teacher conferences:

"IT ALL MAKES SO MUCH SENSE NOW!"

You know you're a teacher if
you hear these 3 questions at
least 1,000 times a year:

1. What page are we on?
2. Do we have to write in complete sentences?
3. Can I borrow a pencil?

YOU KNOW YOU'RE A TEACHER . . .

There are many ways to define a teacher. Whether it's by the way they talk, the way they walk, the clothes they wear, or the things they cherish most in life, teachers are a unique type of human being. You know you're a teacher if...

- If comfort has taken precedence over fashion in your shoe closet.

- If you can tell how long someone has been teaching by the amount of marker on their hands.

- If you wish bladder control, shoe tying, walking backward, and laminating were skills you could put on your resume.

- If you've ever considered locking yourself in a dark storage closet, just to eat lunch for 5 minutes in silence.

- If you can memorize the names of over 100 new students in a week, but you can't memorize the cell-phone number you've had for over a year.

- When it's Monday afternoon and you've already lost your voice. And your sanity. And all your brand-new markers.

- If you ignore anyone who doesn't raise their hand before speaking. Even your friends and family sometimes.

- When seeing "your" instead of "you're" on Facebook makes you cringe.

- When the idea of laminating on a Sunday afternoon gives you butterflies in your stomach.

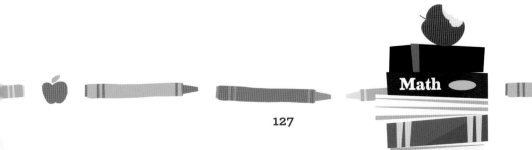

DEDICATION/ACKNOWLEDGMENTS

This book is dedicated to all the educators around the world who devote (or have devoted) their lives to making the world a better place, one child, one student, one day at a time. May you always find laughter in the trials and tribulations of the teaching profession, and always remember: you're only human, and you're awesome. Thank you for everything you sacrifice to shine the light for others. There aren't enough coffee mugs, apples, chocolates, and crayon wreaths in the world to show you the appreciation you so rightfully deserve. Mankind is eternally grateful.